The Marriage Killers

Book Three of:
"I Guess I Do" The Ultimate
Marriage Survival Guide

BEN DONLEY

Jock and Lola Publishing

The Coast in Beverly Hills, CA 90210

The Windmill Ranch in Snyder, TX 79550

Copyright © 2014

Printed in the United States of America

Dedicated to My Person

Foreword by
The Grim Reaper

As someone who has been a death and dying expert for thousands of years, I want to say that this book is exactly what is needed so that couples can avoid the cruel swipe of my relational scythe. (Most people think I kill only the body, but I took up the hobby of killing marriages a long time ago and statistics show that I've gotten pretty good at it.) Anyway, I got married recently myself, and I've got to admit that making marriage work is far harder than I imagined it would be. I've pissed Mrs. Reaper off more times than I can count by breaking many of the commandments set out by my good friend and author of this book, Ben Donley.

When he asked me to write the foreword, I actually jumped at the chance to do so, because as a married, cloaked and skeleton-like killer who never thought he had a chance to land a mate, I have joined the light and desire for as many of the living to understand it is not I who is the main cause of their marriage funerals; they are the problems. It is because of their stupid actions and inactions, which they do nothing about, that are causing unnecessary divorces.

Please, married couples, I beg you with all of my dead heart to heed the words of this book so that you don't move from the altar to anger to an underground plot with a headstone above your heads.

That's all I have for now. I'll be seeing you at some point (some of you sooner than others) but in the meantime let's agree to work at our marriages to avoid early deaths and to make our love much less grim.

Sincerely,

The G.R.

Preface

I Guess I Do: The Ultimate Marriage Survival Guide—Marriage Killers is the third book in a trilogy of self-help relationship books.

This three book series aims to challenge every reader:

⬦ To do some major pre-marital preparation by asking the Frequently UnAnswered Questions (FUAQs) before a wedding ceremony happens.

⬦ To make use of the best relational practices once you have tied the knot so that you end up being a marriage winner rather than one of the ever-growing 60% who divorce.

⬦ To avoid the major and minor "marriage killers," which abound in most homes across this country and beyond.

**This relationship series is unlike anything you have ever read in that it tackles those topics most other relationship books fail to touch (and does so in fierce but fun ways). Prepare to laugh, to squirm, to discover, and to vastly improve on your side of the spousal equation.

Acknowledgements

Special thanks go out to all of the following humans who have helped with this marriage guide.

◇ Marianne Randals, my partner in business and literary crime.

◇ Kevin Rhoads for being a superstar friend and designer.

◇ Connie Nugent for being a genius editor.

◇ My book ambassadors and reviewers on Amazon.

◇ All of the couples who have allowed me to learn from them as they prepared for, suffered from, and even enjoyed marriage while in my presence.

◇ Jock and Lola Publishing Group for being a powerful launching pad into this ever-changing literary world of ours.

◇ My A-Team

Who is this book written for?

Serious Couples who don't want "marriage vultures" to ever circle above their relationship.

Humble People who actually want to work at doing the smart things and avoiding the stupid things.

Honest People who like taking an honest look at their idiosyncrasies, habits, and stupidities with a bent toward evolving beyond them.

Wives who do not want their bouquets thrown onto a relational gravesite.

Husbands who don't want to melt the Unity Candle down into just another ball of wax.

Lovers who don't want the small things to stack up, crush their hearts, and separate them into two warring parties led by hungry divorce lawyers.

Partners who don't want to bury their marriage memories under a head stone.

Welcome to Book Three!!!
R.I.P.PING Marriage

It is so, so, so, so super easy to screw up a marriage relationship. And I'm not saying *screw up* in ways that can be fixed by a therapist. I am instead talking about a Quentin Tarantino-esque weaponry-based hatred where you are being regularly nudged to go ahead and pre-purchase a headstone so you can etch the epitaph and mark the dates of the relationship's birth and violent death.

There are at least one thousand actions/inactions we can do/ not do that will draw us closer and closer to this sort of marital carnage. This book is all about these little killers, which I recommend you pay attention to if you don't want to strangle the air out of your vows. Some are funny. Some are dead serious. But all of them are dangerous. Ignore them at your peril.

Let me introduce you to the King Ben Version of the Marriage Commandments. Over 100 wise advisements and 39 *Thou Shalt Nots* are here for your enjoyment and safety.

Ready or not, here they come...

Table of Contents

Thou Shalt Not:

Number One
Thou Shalt Not:
Say the following things to your spouse:

◇ I forbid you to _____

◇ I wish you were more like _____

◇ I make all of the money and you should be thankful I give you an allowance.

◇ You are very pear-shaped.

◇ I've never really loved you.

◇ I'm not *in love* with you anymore.

◇ You are my biggest mistake/You are my biggest regret.

◇ I knew I should have married _____.

◇ I wish you would die/I poisoned the Frosted Flakes you just ate.

◇ I hate you.

◇ Don't touch me ever again.

◇ I hope our kids are nothing like you/look nothing like you.

◇ You bore me.

◇ I trust my mother's/father's opinion more than yours.

◇ I think you are worthless/a waste of space.

◇ Act your age/You are so immature/You are such a baby.

◇ Your parents really screwed you up.

◇ I despise your parents in every way.

◇ Does your PMS ever end? (has been used "effectively" for both sexes).

◇ I do not recall you having such huge hips (again, has been used "effectively" for both sexes).

◇ I faked it every time ("effective" but harder to prove for one of the sexes).

◇ Your head/teeth are way too big for your body.

◇ I might have Chlamydia.

◇ It didn't mean anything. It was purely physical.

◇ Whenever you die, I will probably marry again soon.

◇ I'm wearing your underwear.

Number Two
Thou Shalt Not:
Become the influential, caring listener for a wounded person of the opposite sex or counsel a person of the opposite sex about their marriage problems

So many extra-marital affairs begin in a fairly innocent manner with one nice person acting as the compassionate, listening ear for a married person who "needs" to share about his/her life struggles and/or marriage disappointment.

Don't be that nice person.

Don't be that compassionate, listening ear.

Sure, the wounded and/or disappointed married people might have some very real hurts, a super sad *backstory* and even legitimate complaints about their wives/husbands. And if so, they actually do *need* to talk to someone. But unless you are a professional therapist who has been trained to set up proper client boundaries, understands how to maintain emotional distance and is being paid by a married person to counsel him/her towards better understanding and direction, you are a terrible choice.

Even if you have been told that you are extremely gifted in advising others, that you are the best listener in town, you are madly in love with your own spouse, are not attracted to the other person and hate the very idea of cheating/adultery, you should extricate thyself from the potential dangers of an unpredictable situation where emotions and private relational details are at the foundation of a very familiar deconstruction.

I'm issuing the strongest warning I can here: Do not think you are the exception to the rules of engagement in this situation.

DIS-ENGAGE in 5-4-3-2-1...

Wounded, troubled and "unloved" people have a tendency to cling to someone who shows them real empathy and care. And while you may not fall for them, feel any attraction to them, or even choke a little bit in what you do or say to them, you cannot guarantee that another person's interpretation of your caring, listening, and advising will be correct. When people are in difficult mental and emotional situations, they are often feeling especially insecure and seeking another person who will make them feel better about themselves.

Do not be their insecurity-cure and they will neither tell their spouses about how they wish they had someone more like you nor will they become a stalker who fantasizes about your becoming their huggy-bear and security blanket.

You will also keep yourself from thinking of this other person as a temporary option if and when your own marriage picks up some "killer hitchhikers."

I have had my own stalker before because I am nice and caring (and dashingly humble). And I can assure you, while it seemed cool at the initial stages to have someone show fresh interest in me, offer me compliments, and present me the open invitation to their body-party, it can go past happy-groupie time fairly fast and head toward Glenn Close in *Fatal Attraction* if you do not off-ramp it immediately. (You never know who has some "true crazy" in them.)

Keep those persons far away from you and your marriage or you might face what can become an addictive decay.

Do you hear me?

Will you obey my instructions or play with the fire?

If you are a relational-pyro, just know that this deep burn will be as painful as ten Roman Candles shot into your buttocks while habanero peppers are jammed into your eyeballs. (That's meant to be a deterrent by the way—not an encouragement for you sadists among my readership.)

.

Number Three
Thou Shalt Not:
Become a Social Media Polygamist

If you are married to a physical 3-D spouse in the regular world, you are not allowed to build flirty, intimate, secret-sharing, spouse-bashing, body part showing and/or TMI relationships with people of the opposite sex who appear on various social media outlets. Basically, you are not allowed to go on long-distance emotional dating sprees with those whom you have not married in the real world.

Sure, I know it seems "innocent" and "harmless" to re-invent yourself to a population of men/women who are starving for your pixilated pheromones and Insta-grammed (and probably Photoshopped) head shots. I know having an e-harem of Pinterest, Twitter, and Facebook boy/girlfriends can be a fun escape from the mundane world of being married to an actual person who is in your face 24-7 (a person who usually does not limit their words to 140 characters). Having fifteen online lovers you can choose from for some dopamine fixes when they *like, retweet, comment on* and make you out to be a sexy, funny genius can make you feel like a King or a Queen instead of a diaper changer and toilet plunger for the actual spouse who has stopped caring about showcasing his/her good side.

But it ain't cool. It's fantasy. It's social media polygamy and unless you have a Mormon hard drive, you should not be engaging in it.

Why?

Because relationships demand the real, not some false outreaches to computerized desperation cases. Marriage does not allow for some promised adorations for an Icelandic creative writer who you think might actually be your faraway soul mate, because they "get you as you really are." Give me a break, humanoid. You don't live in the fictionalized world of humans in love with vampires who cannot be had. You have got to stop dreaming; cut off your online relationships and start investing in the real one you have.

Super major warnings to certain groups of E-polygamists:

*If you are married and have any open accounts on E-harmony, Match.com, or any such sites, where you are pretending to be unmarried simply to get emotionally propped up by someone outside of your sphere of responsibility, you deserve to be dumped. If you are that insecure and emotionally unstable, tell your spouse about it and let him/her walk away from your *sad state of affairs*. Then, send me an email about it and I'll make sure to hack into your dating profile and make you look as appealing as Jay Leno in a string bikini.

*If you are married and you play avatar-based online games and you have actually allowed your elf to get married to some handsome/sexy sort of gnome, you need to book an appointment with someone who will use appropriate levels of open-handed violence to lead you to online game divorce.

Show some respect. Live in the real-world. Escape through activities instead of fake people love on World of Warcraft.

Number Four
Thou Shalt Not:
Leave the bathroom door open or unlocked whilst taking a dump

After the second week of marital life and until three weeks ago, I started leaving the bathroom door open so that my wife could enter and do her multi-tasked morning readiness while I took a poop. I now admit this was a bad decision that I allowed to go on for far too long.

When we were dating, there was no way I would have ever allowed her to see my skinny little thighs perched on top of the porcelain pot as I attempted to read Sports Illustrated and wipe my butt with perfection.

But after we pledged our lives to one another, I gave in to her pleadings for free entry to use the big mirror/bathroom sink and we started having real life conversations while I shot fecal matter out of a once private orifice. There she came - into my sacred space while casually putting on mascara and combing her hair while I crapped with the force of a jet engine. Even with attempted restraint, I could not turn this *butt dump* into a polite moment—not with the stench of dead mammals, rotten sauerkraut, and intestinal napalm being wafted up from my bent thighs and floating into the nose of my lovely bride as she flossed. (The Grim Reaper was even forced unconscious in the bathtub.)

Why is this not at least a marital misdemeanor?

For those who are wondering, you can know with certainty that there is absolutely nothing sexy about my semi-curled-up body, ripping puffy Charmin from a shiny toilet paper roller. I am instead the non-sexy and non-muscular husband on a hard, white seat with a crunched-up face attempting to muffle excessive voluble farting so as not to interrupt a spousal conversation about Wells Fargo bill-pays that need to be made. My lighting some matches and trying to maintain some sort of eye contact just does not make everything okay.

I actually think I would rather have a complete stranger come in and discuss the meaning of life with me in this insecure position than the one who is my lover. Since I barely see my wife anyway due to weird work schedules, I do not want this gross and gruesome image of me to be her brain's profile "my husband picture" that pops up as a contrast image against all the other males she sees during her day.

So, I don't care what anyone says: **Marriage Mystery should be maintained inside this room.**

"Crapping" (the scientific term) is a non-plural activity, an individual Constitutional Right (Maintaining the Separation between Poop and Mate) that allows for some respect to remain between husband and wife. Thus, I lock the door now and do not let my wife inside when I am having my own 911 Booty Call.

Sure it makes her mad that it takes us longer to get ready in the morning, but I think she is starting to forget how gross I can be, which is a lot more important. Poor punctuality does not come close to the crime of trying to act cool while in the act of self-relief.

Let's flip this over to show equality to the sexes: There ain't no lady on the planet who poops pleasantly.

I know this to be logical and thus I refuse to enter in to the toilet room when my wife *supposedly* delivers the old #2 - aka hot, baked brownies. (I like to imagine that my wife never unleashes the rocky mudslide but *if* she does, I want to hold onto hope that her very limited amount of intestinal waste rides out like golden rockets on the backs of bright white unicorns and smelling of Cinnabon.)

You see, I *will* keep my wife's beauty in the front of my mind and not dialogue with her about pop culture as she grunts out a pound of old food. This enables me to keep her in my head as the one I said "I do" to instead of thinking of her as the "doo-doo lady."

Reality in this case is unnecessary. What I refuse to believe won't hurt me in this case. And it won't kill her.

Number Five
Thou Shalt Not:
Allow your breath to become a
weapon of mass destruction

In the olden days, I used to vigorously brush not only my teeth but also all the mini shingles on the roof of my mouth and every square millimeter of my tongue before I went on any sort of date with my girlfriend so that my breath would be very fresh and inviting. I even carried a hidden toothbrush and toothpaste around so I could freshen up the reachable parts of my esophageal tract after dinner. I also had strong minty gum, Listerine tongue strips, Tic-Tacs, and Altoids in my pocket to ensure airflow happiness from my mouth to her nose.

You could have called me the King of Oral Hygiene.

Once marriage happened to this same *girlfriend*, I got lazier and lazier with the mouth care and became careless. Whereas once I might have qualified for membership in "Dental Mensa", I stopped brushing the taste buds as often and left my high-level hygiene IQ at the altar. I stopped investing in breath saving insurance coverage. I gave up on scrapers and floss. My pie-hole became an unpredictable and even dangerous cavern for emission.

Without my genius-level oral prevention and protection, my mouth could no longer be trusted as girl-friendly. It quickly became known as a "suspected terrorist wearing a strap-on bomb shirt made of strong coffee aftertaste, Wasabi-laced sea-weed sushi, Slim Jims, and Onion Ring blow-ups." I was carrying around a tongue equipped with mass destruction abilities.

Basically I became a regular nostril strangler.

Sure, I would toss in a tiny piece of ineffective Trident gum to mask it, but that gum stood no chance against brownish-green taste buds to go along with the "yellow death metal" on the curvy top of my mouth and entire throat passage.

Now you might not think this sounds like that big of a deal, but it is. Regularly occurring vile, stinky breath piping out from your mouth lets everyone around know you prefer distance from them. You are letting them know if they want to have a conversation with you, it must be done on the phone or outside of six feet. Nobody appreciates having to throw on a gas mask to be near someone. Most of us know this simple rule and for the sake of our careers and friendships, we take care to do the old "breath in hand" check, followed by breath improvement techniques.

We may not always be spear-minty, but we must always be at a solid distance from having a zombie mouth.

In marriage, we tend to lose this hygiene basic at the worst time. Married people are supposed to kiss one another. But if one or both of you is not being careful with your breath, those kisses are going to be gone pretty soon.

If I were my wife, I would not kiss me most of the time. She does not need to have my *unkempt tongue* enter her space, much less her mouth. And it goes the other way too. If my hot little lady has peanut butter and Ranch flavored Corn Nut breath, I am going to call a flagrant technical foul on her. Maybe suspend her from my personal space for three days until the floss and tongue spoon are resurrected from the bathroom drawer.

Is this shallow? Probably. But it is a real problem.

Why?

This is a huge point that you really need to memorize and have tattooed onto your frontal cortex:

> **Marriages can drown in the shallow just as easily as in the deep. The small things can kill a relationship as easily as the big things.**

(Just in case you were wondering, the above point is really the major underlying idea that drives this book's existence. Small things in marriage are not insignificant. Sometimes they are the camel straws and the last *Jenga* pulls to make a marriage fall.)

Okay, back to this specific "small thing."

If I want my wife to be within three feet of me in conversation, I need to return to some of my pre-marital exhalations. If I want to be greeted with a kiss, I have to get back to my roots. **I have to re-do unto my wife what I want done unto me. It's the Golden Marriage Rule applied to your mouth mechanisms.**

And because I care so much about you, I have included a couple of other vital lists on the following pages that will help you become less physically offensive.

***Below is a list of foods/drinks that *cannot be consumed* without a solid four-minute mouth scrubdown with the appropriate equipment (toothbrush, powerful toothpaste, tongue scraper, a Scope-like liquid throat burner and if you are a true Casanova, Cherry Pop Rocks). Behold—"The No-No No Kissy List"

◇ Any flavor of Corn Nut or sunflower seed

◇ Coffee, cappuccino, espresso, etc.

◇ Tortilla chips (add two minutes to the abovementioned scrub if they happen to be Cool Ranch chips)

◇ Every version of Cheeto or Funyun

◇ Garlic bread or garlic anything

◇ Peanuts in any form

◇ Salad Dressings

◇ Sashimi, sushi, sushi rolls and pretty much any fish-based concoction

◇ Kombucha and all health food store drinks (namely apple cider vinegar)

◇ Red Bulls, Monsters and all other energy drinks made up of unknown cosmic chemicals and elk blood

◇ Onion rings

◇ Milk

*There are certainly others but I think I've covered the most common *butt-breath creating* culprits. If you eat or drink any of the above and you are not at home, you better have a covert *breath-improvement bag* nearby that you can access. I am not recommending a fanny pack, but having a tailor sew some pockets into your underwear or panties would be pretty sweet. Or transforming a gun holder into a hygiene holster might not be a bad idea. You could be known as the *Sheriff of Smell* on Facebook if you like.

Number Six
Thou Shalt Not:
French kiss your spouse with untamed morning breath

Since this one is very close to the topic introduced so well on the last few pages, I will not go into details about these details. But, I have to make this a separate topic because too many couples I've spoken with think that to kiss each other on the lips upon waking is a good way to show their significant other they are connecting from the beginning of each day.

Did those couples that have decided on this have some sort of *morning breath surgery*, which makes their early A.M. mouths and tongues smell like lavender and honey rather than stinking like diarrhea and rigor mortis?

I think not.

I'll bet my bankroll that their morning breath is the same as the rest of the world's morning breath, which ranges from upper case BAD to upper case POOP ON A STICK.

Anyway, let's carry this morning breath assumption forward and project it onto you, the reader. Your tongue is on the nasty continuum somewhere, which means it is very, very bad until you beat it back with pre-mentioned implements of dental wonder. Thus, you must not kiss your spouse when you wake up unless it is on the back of their middle spine. Do not lean over and put your semi-open lips near their semi-open lips.

Why?

Sleep is probably the worst thing that ever happened to human breath since the invention of Slim Jims and garlic toast. And so, if you do the lean over and press your lips and God forbid press your tongue into the open mouth (read: gaping grave) of your morning spouse, you are not connecting to your significant other or building daylong intimacy; you are instead showing your foolish desire to taste a spastic colon. You are also subjecting your supposed loved one to a waking *Nightmare on Help Me Street*.

Just because actors in Hollywood movies wake up and immediately start making out does not mean they are good examples for you. At home, David Beckham wakes up with ass-breath and would not dare make out with an awakening Posh Spice (Victoria), who also has breath from the depths of Hell. And if he does, he should be treated like the bendable criminal he surely would be.

Are you hearing me, couples? Tune your guitar before taking it out onto the stage. And if you have a bedside blowtorch to cauterize your tongue, you are my hero.

Number Seven
Thou Shalt Not:
Assume you are a Great Kisser/
Be a Terrible Kisser

Okay, just because you don't kiss your spouse without first dealing a crushing blow to food-borne or sleep-borne putridity, does not mean you are out of the woods when it comes to the very crucial skill set involved in kissing someone.

I don't know about you, but I was never required to take kissing lessons. I was made to take dance lessons and was given the opportunity to take tennis and golf lessons. But my parents never had the foresight to hire some well-dusted widow in her mid-70's to come to my house and teach me how to kiss. I was left with a book my brother loaned me entitled, *How to Kiss with Confidence*. And while the paperback was a valuable read from the fifth grade forward (it gave me the reputation as one of the top three kissers for my age range among one hundred smart young ladies who were polled), it did not take me into the advanced dimensions of lip service.

Sun Tzu was once overheard on the battlefield saying, "Kissing is an art rarely studied and never perfected." Or maybe it was a quote from a wise Shih-Tzu puppy that spoke to Joaquin Phoenix while he was on a peyote journey in Arizona. Regardless of the source, the saying is true.

Kissing is not just the placement of your lips on someone else's face (and sometimes body). Kissing is not just crossing into someone's personal space and going lip-to-lip or tongue-to-tongue. Kissing requires proper head angling, synchronized hand placements, excellent overall timing, appropriate tongue mimicry, best breath pauses, slobber control, soft lip balming, romantic eye contacting, intuitive intensification, tooth control, and a bunch of other key multitasks that will transform someone from a dangerous mouth intruder into a trusted lip-master. I don't have the pages to be your sensei right now. But, maybe your town has *tongue yoga* classes you can attend. Check your city's Google Places and sign up today. Or just call the local community center for tutoring services.

Number Eight
Thou Shalt Not:
Insist that your way is "the right way" when there are actually multiple, viable options in getting something done.

Sometimes there is only one way to do something, or to get somewhere or to respond to a question. But most of the time, there is more than one way to handle something or someone. Sure, one specific way might be proved to be the most efficient, easiest, or fastest way to do something. But it is actually rare that the "one way" argument is anything more than a claim based on people's experiences, their limited comparative attempts, their level of comfort, and their sense of timing when it comes to making debate with others that their chosen ways are right, or even better, best.

An example: You are driving to the grocery store and decide to take a left at the stop sign so you can get onto the freeway, which will ultimately take you to an exit that will allow you to do a U-turn and then into the grocery store parking lot so you can purchase a few tasty items for your refrigerator. The problem comes when other people in the car insist that you go right at the stop sign, avoid the freeway, race through neighborhoods and go into the parking lot on the backside of the store because it is faster and better.

Faster and better?

"Really, my gentle lover?"

Are they sure? Have they timed it? And if they have, why did they time it? And if they timed it, was it at this exact time of day? Did they even time it on the same day of the week? And, even if they did time it perfectly on numerous occasions and have on hand a fully stocked book comparing the two routes for every day, every date, and every time range and can prove to you that their way was is truly "faster and better," how much faster and better is it? Will it save you an hour? Will it help you avoid daily vehicular manslaughter charges? If not, who cares?

And why do they think they can tell you, the chosen and capable driver who has passed the necessary tests to earn a license, how to get somewhere that has multiple directional options? Doesn't the driver get to choose? Isn't that in the Constitution? It should be.

Is this just an exercise in control? Does it qualify for minor spousal abuse?

This same problem can be applied to many other common marital situations: How to do the dishes; How to put the sheets on the bed; How to control your weight; How to deal with people; How to shop efficiently; How to act in public; How to dress for success; How to wear the hair; How to write emails; How to decorate your office; How to set the proper volume on the TV set; How to pay bills; How to use toilet paper; How to paint the walls; How to hold the baby's head; How to use shortcut keys on the computer; How to store your boarding pass; How to smile for photos; How to microwave popcorn; How to recycle; How to dance; How to change the light bulb; How to clone a sheep; How to hypnotize a rich person; How to dispose of a body; etc.

The list seems to goes on and on (doesn't it) for people who think they have a monopoly on all the right ways. Opinionated spouses, even those with some measure of experience or proof to back their ways, are uncool and not fun to be around.

If you happen to be one of these spouses who always have their mouths open jabbering away about the proper way your partner needs to operate when he/she has myriad options to accomplish whatever is being done, here is the main thing you need to remember: *Unless your partner specifically asks for your help or gives you carte-blanche permission to advise them on the right way or the best way or the most effective way, don't say anything to them*—especially if they happen to be "driving." This advice includes non-verbal communication. You should not squirm, roll your eyes, furrow your brow, cross your arms on your chest, do the long sigh or shake your head from side to side.

Why?

Because every time you insist that your way is right and best, you are also saying that your partner's way is wrong or stupid or foolish or ineffective or inefficient.

Is that what you are trying to do?

If so, why would you want to blast away at your loved one's confidence and decisiveness?

Are you trying to put your partner in his/her place and force him/her into a controlled humility?

Or is it that you have to be the smartest person in every room? Are you trying to prove something to yourself or to someone else?

Hopefully you just don't realize you are doing it and will now stop!?! And if you decide to stop, I'm not very worried about you; I'm sure you know the best way to bring this annoying habit to a halt.

Number Nine
Thou Shalt Not:
Laugh at your spouse when he or she gets hurt

Everybody likes a good laugh. And admittedly, it is pretty difficult to keep from laughing when you see someone close to you do
something stupid, which leads to a minor injury. It's definitely
not easy to quell a chuckle when your spouse tumbles over after
trying to sit down where there was no chair. When he does something clumsy like this, it's fine to smirk and even laugh a bit as you
help him get away from a simple bruised ego.

But, it is not cool to laugh at your spouse when he/she does something stupid or even accidental, which actually causes injury. My
wife used to die laughing when I would hurt myself due to the
high-pitched squeals and shrieks that typically accompanied my
painful acts of foolishness. And while I do look back with the help
of therapy and recognize that she could not help herself because
I did sound like a wounded banshee the time I scalded my hand
with Starbucks coffee and hit my face while doing a swan dive
into bottom of a pool, I still think she might have controlled
how hard she laughed as well as minimized the timeframe. Two
minutes of knee-slapping and shriek impersonation as my flesh
cooked or eyes blackened would have probably been better than
five minutes.

Anyway, I am going to go ahead and make a short list of things
that you must not laugh at your spouse for.

No laughing when spouse:

◇ Trips over a raised piece of sidewalk in flip-flops, especially if an exposed toe smashes directly into the cement and/or spouse goes sprawling onto her elbows in front of a Starbucks window.

◇ Bites his tongue while simultaneously eating and talking to friends over lunch or dinner. Sure it is fairly funny when your spouse stops mid-sentence, grabs his face in anguish and lets out a wail after screwing up a fairly basic human body control. But if you have ever bitten your tongue, you must remember the harsh feeling of putting teeth to mouth muscle.

◇ Staples a finger to a thick set of papers.

◇ Burns a hand with a hot iron (waffle or clothes).

◇ Chomps down on an existing canker sore or cold sore.

◇ Hammers fingers while trying to pound in a nail.

◇ Runs over a foot with the lawnmower.

◇ Falls off of a ladder changing a light bulb or putting up Christmas lights.

◇ Puts a hand into an oscillating fan.

◇ Accidentally squeezes ProActiv instead of saline into eyes.

◇ Steps on a freshly broken piece of a drinking glass.

◇ Slips getting out of the shower.

◇ Bangs the head falling out bed in the middle of the night.

◇ Pulls the lower back trying to pull off a 1980's dance move.

◇ Slices a face or leg or armpit while shaving.

◇ Takes a foul ball to the face.

◇ Tears rotator cuff while bowling.

◇ Flies off of a fast moving treadmill.

◇ Flip bounces off of a trampoline while playing Crack the Egg.

◇ Semi-electrocutes self while using a faulty plug.

◇ Stabs self with scrapbooking scissors.

◇ Slaughters a hand with the cheese grater.

◇ Topples from stiletto heels and sprains ankle.

◇ Takes a Frisbee in the nose.

That covers most of the stuff I have faced in my marriage. Now we move to the crucial How-to:

How can you stop the laughing from happening when these above events occur?

Option 1: Read *Clockwork Orange* and make special note of how young Alex got "cured" of his ultra-violence. Then apply those methods to yourself by watching Chris Farley movies/skits and stabbing yourself in the leg with a pocketknife every time the late actor hurts himself.

Better Option 2: Put yourself in your spouse's shoes before anything happens and think about what it's like to be laughed at for anything. Being laughed at is hard to handle, especially when you make a dumb move leading to pain. If you would not like that sort of response, especially from someone who is supposed to have the most compassion for you, then force yourself to put on a sad face when you see the event happen, show some care, make sure he/she is okay and then run to a soundproof closet so you can replay the scene in your mind and laugh hysterically.

Number Ten
𝕿𝖍𝖔𝖚 𝕾𝖍𝖆𝖑𝖙 𝕹𝖔𝖙:
Be a Serial Incompleter

There are so many simple, recurring tasks/chores lounging all around your marriage relationship and they all need to be completed. These revolving chores are fairly obvious to anyone who is half paying attention. Let me address a few for those of you who don't know what I am talking about.

The car runs out of gas regularly. Most cars have a built-in warning system that comes on when the vehicle gets low on fuel. If not a light or a beep or a robot lady explaining the need to stop at a gas station, every car has a dashboard tool with a bright needle that moves from F (representing Full) towards E (representing Empty). When this needle gets near the E or the robot woman warns, or the light flashes on, you need to take on the annoying (and extremely easy) task of pulling into the outdoor, shaded lane of a convenient neighborhood gas station and bring the car back to Fullness! Don't be the spouse who realizes the car is almost out of fuel but drives past about fifteen stations and pulls the car into the garage so that your spouse can take care of this duty later. **Gas Incompleters** are lazy punks.

Did you know that the laundry basket is where clothes are supposed to go rather than onto the floor? (First things first, get that truth into your behaviors and pull your panties and Underoos up and off the restroom tiles.)

Moving on to the more crucial point, after several days of both spouses utilizing underwear, socks, shirts, blouses, jeans, pants, skirts, kilts, etc., the laundry basket should be filling up. There is no warning on the laundry basket like there is with a car that tells you this hamper is moving from E to F. But, since you will find yourself placing your own sweaty body coverings into that hamper in the morning and maybe even in the evening, you probably have the sense to notice when the clothes container is starting to belch out its contents. A good sign of this is when the lid of the hamper will not shut because there are so many clothes pressed into it.

Now, when you spot this vital sign of laundry fullness, do not do what is super tempting. Do not use all your force to jam the overflowing clothing down towards the bottom of the hamper making it seem like the point of fullness hasn't actually been reached. (This classic **Dirty Clothes Incompleter** technique usually makes use of forceful shoves by the hands and shoulders, but the advanced means of avoidance leads the lazy spouse to find a way to jump down from a higher space onto the bulging clothes stack with their feet, thus making use of full body weight to press out all remaining air space that was existing between the clothing pieces.)

Shame, shame, we know your name, clothes-smashers. All that extra effort you put into keeping the laundry process incomplete could have been used to save your spouse from having to separate the clothes into proper piles and wash and dry armloads of stuff. Your only chance to save your good name at that pitiable point is for you to take on the "folding, drawer-ing and re-hanging clothes" duties. If you neglect these final stages as well by walking past the stacks of newly cleaned clothes over and over until your spouse does a neat job of it all, you should be Bounced.

I don't want to go into that much detail about everything else on the marital list of repeating chores. But I at least want to make a list of those things you need to help Complete.

◇ Dirty dishes are not supposed to be left around the house.

◇ Dirty dishes are not supposed to be left in the sink unscrubbed.

◇ A full dishwasher should not be left alone until your spouse realizes there are no clean forks or spoons.

◇ A dishwasher full of newly washed and dried plates and bowls should be emptied and its contents placed back in their pre-determined homes.

◇ A laptop computer running on fumes because you have been surfing on it all day, should not be shut and left unplugged. Power it up.

◇ When that computer sends you critical auto-update warnings, don't push the "Later" button.

◇ When the toilet paper supply in the restroom hits the "half of one roll" mark, it is time for a Completer to bring in two full rolls of Charmin.

◇ If a toilet paper roll actually runs out of sheets on your turn, remove the toilet paper holder, discard the used cardboard, place a new toilet paper roll on the holder and put the holder firmly back in place. A good Completer will even get the roll started so that it has spin-momentum for the next sitter.

◇ Mail in the mailbox should be brought into the house and separated into junk mail, his mail, and her mail. Junk mail is ripped into pieces and thrown into the trash.

◇ You know you can smell the baby's dirty diaper when it is loaded with poop. It's an unmistakable malodorous reality. When the smell emanates into your nostrils, do not fake like you have an important cell phone call to take and hand off your stinky child to your spouse. As well, do not use the alternative evasion technique of Febrezing your child's outer diaper or taping a Pine Tree Car Freshener to the baby's back so that the smell can be minimized until you can place the child into a crib and make your getaway.

◇ Feed your pet/clean up its crap or don't have a pet.

These are but a few of the recurring incomplete things that should be given attention by both spouses. If you are an Incompleter, please push the volume down on your laziness, turn off the chore evasion switch and just finish up some tasks, which are crying out for you to do your part.

Number Eleven
Thou Shalt Not:
Be Reactionary with Counseling

My theory: Every couple, no matter how solid they are, requires a wise third party to act as a *backstory-knowing* inquisitor and compassionate emotional vampire who is allowed to bite into the vulnerable parts of their relationship. But, most couples do not ever enter into counseling until they "have to."

What are they waiting for?

Many couples stall until they near a breaking point built on years of frustration and find themselves standing on the brink of separation or divorce. They wait until it gets so bad or so intolerable that they cannot salvage any semblance of joyful union on their own. They speak only in fighting words and see one another only as burdensome.

Why do people think of counseling only as crisis-based? Why do couples finally react only as their marriage gets close to a finish line rather than proactively seeking counseling as a preventive measure?

I think it has a lot to do with the following:

> A lot of individuals do not like to tell a complete stranger about their histories, especially if those histories are dotted with embarrassing or hard times. Therapists typically ask questions about such things and are not easily fooled or evaded.

Many couples do not want to rehash their "love story" and talk about how it is going unless they feel that they must. After all, who wants to bring up junk that will just lead them to fight in front of someone else? Who wants to hire a referee when it's only the first few rounds of marriage? When it gets bloody and MMA-style or at least past King Hippo, then it might be time to share a bit with someone else.

Since it costs money, it is often seen as an unnecessary expense unless divorce, which costs a lot more, pops its head into the scene.

Counseling takes time and energy and requires vulnerability and honesty. Most couples are already tired and cannot fathom dishing out fresh emotional juice when they still have a couple of kids to deal with at home.

Counseling can reveal that people have been relational failures in many ways and it can ask them to change their ways, their words, their directions, their reactions, etc. Not too many people want to admit/face their faults. Fewer people want to/know how to change.

Culturally, marriage therapy has been typically regarded as one of the last lines of defense against a divorce. Marriage therapy is considered the landing spot just before the trial separation option. When someone tells someone else that they both are going to marriage therapy, the common assumption is that things must be terrible and the end is nigh. Gossip follows. Uncool.

The common thought for a lot of couples is that they can figure out how to recover their love without a third party. They don't need someone being a marriage crutch. They got into this thing together and they can fix it. This comes down to two people being a bit arrogant. They apparently think they can do better than a well-trained and often wiser therapist who has unbiased advice to inject into old perspectives.

All of the above or at least some of the above keeps couples from regarding counseling as a necessary lifelong budget line item. Truth is, counseling/therapy from the time you get engaged until the casket-time is a total lifeline that will make your marriage grow and prosper. There will be less fighting and clawing to keep it together and more of the healthy preventions to lean upon.

Some of the best advice I can offer: Create a budget that allows for you and your spouse to go to a qualified therapist (you both agree on) once or twice a month every month until you die. It will be one of the greatest investments you could ever make because a third party can hear you both out while setting up a safe structure for regular sharing. A wise third party will always be inserting vital ways for you to improve on what you have built and can be working on the positive movements rather than always trying to undo the negative damage you will do when left to your own two-person perspective.

Number Twelve
Thou Shalt Not:
Use the following excuses:

◇ I was exhausted.

◇ I was drunk.

◇ It just runs in my family.

◇ That's just how I am.

◇ It was too good of a deal/job offer to pass up.

◇ I thought I could outrun him.

◇ I deserved to treat myself.

◇ It's because you never treat me well.

◇ It's because you never speak my true love languages.

◇ I just felt so sorry for them.

◇ I didn't want to hurt your feelings/make you feel insecure.

◇ You started it.

◇ It was an important text.

◇ I read it on Google (e.g., 'Burning Man is for families').

◇ I didn't have time.

◇ I was craving it.

◇ You are better at it than I am.

◇ I just needed a change.

◇ God told me that this was the way for both of us to go.

◇ I was trying to make you happy.

◇ The experts said so.

◇ The risk seemed so small at the time.

◇ I needed to relax.

◇ My mother thought it would be a better idea for us.

◇ That is what I am expected to do.

◇ I couldn't let my buddies down.

Number Thirteen
Thou Shalt Not:
Be an Egg-Sheller

To *walk on eggshells* around someone means you are trying very hard not to upset or offend them. In most cases when I have been told to *walk on eggshells* around someone it is because the person I am about to deal with is such a fragile, easily breakable, and constantly offended human that s/he has earned the reputation for being the worst sort of annoyance imaginable.

Confession: Eggshell people make me want to put on sharp-cleated soccer shoes so I can jump all over their misplaced sensitivities as if they were thick sheets of bubble wrap under my feet. Easily offended people make me want to pound their "touchy" buttons and using a full-force ball peen hammer until they ask for a restraining order against me. (I would welcome a restraining order so I would not even be allowed to go anywhere near their huge clown feet which have toes that cannot help but be stepped on if you are near.)

Keep in mind that I am not speaking about legitimately wounded people who might need special care due to current pain or recent difficulty. I am talking about lifelong whiners who have learned to control their environments and relationships by using some sort of freak-sized, emotional outbreak (anger, withdrawal, hostility, sadness, etc.) that will topple over any sort of normal and balanced situation.

An Egg-Sheller's response to someone's actions, body language, perceived motives, spoken philosophies, opinions, and ideologies (or really to anything they disagree with/threatens their control) is such an overblown and frightening explosion of selfishness, it shrieks loud and clear to a group of people who desire a regular level of collective harmony that extra care must be taken around this person. Egg-Shellers' consistent volatile tantrums make everyone around them know they cannot walk normally when these easily disturbed human beings enter a room if they don't want some sort of loud psycho-breakage to appear.

Thus most people in order *to keep the peace* make a personal decision to be pragmatic and become the most inoffensive and agreeable eggshell-walkers on the planet when in the vicinity of these harmony killers.

Now, what happens when a pragmatic and harmonious person marries a vicious Egg-Sheller?

Train Wreck? Shuttle Explosion? Multiple Spontaneous Combustions?

No. Those would be the accurate descriptors of what happens when one Egg-Sheller marries another Egg-Sheller and both try to use their proclaimed fragilities to control the other. Let me assure you that you do not even want to go to dinner with this marriage combo.

No, when a harmony lover marries an Egg-Sheller, it resembles one quietly whimpering person being led around on a short, painful leash by another person who is barking out rough commands to "sit," "stay," "play dead," and mainly "do as I say."

And this sort of *opposites attract* situation is so common it makes me wonder why—Why is this combination such a common link-up?

It is as if the Egg-Sheller has some sort of GPS specifically designed to locate the most easygoing, peace loving, indecisive, non-boat rocking, harmony lovers in the vicinity.

But that is not the point here. I am not going to go into the psychologies of Egg-Sheller and prey.

The main points here are:

1. Stop being an Egg-Sheller Spouse if you are one. Sure, you may be the true, number one *victim of life* who thinks you deserve a world where no one says "no" to you or disturbs your peace. But, to drag someone into *this* impossible-to-please existence is punitive and mean. Stay single, go see a psychiatrist, get on proper meds, and stop being such a high-maintenance, manipulative person before you get into a lifelong relationship. It is so not okay to be acting the way that you act. It's downright madness.

2. If you are a harmony-at-all-costs person who has married an Egg-Sheller, stop being such a boundary-less wimpsteak of a person who thinks that to tiptoe around someone with emotional control equals love. Set healthy boundaries. Let your Egg-Sheller know that you are not going to allow crazy behavior to go unchecked any longer. Get tougher. Sure, your precious Egg-Sheller may go bonkers on you with intimidations, threats, wailing tears and/or violent tantrums, but you might be the only one who can get him/her to realize that this is not correct behavior. Also, get into therapy yourself. Find out why you were attracted to such a mentally ill manipulator in the first place and why you think you still deserve the punishment that comes with putting up with someone whom no one else wants to deal with.

3. If Egg-Shellers won't seek help or will not stop insisting on environments that they deem fair and necessary but which are actually abusive, you should separate from them until they get some major help or until they agree to enter into some sort of counseling with you.

Number Fourteen
Thou Shalt Not:
a. Give each other cutesy nicknames
b. Give each other evil nicknames
c. Name each other's private parts
d. Use any of the above three names in public conversations

These all fit within the same theme so I will briefly cover them all under the same commandment.

Most cute nicknames are gross and should not be dragged into the public sphere. Sweetheart/Sweetie and baby/babe are fine. Honey, Dear, and Darling work as well. Doll is old school and is okay but it is to be used sparingly because you are neither Mae West nor Clark Gable.

But Cherry-Bear, Grape-Koala or any other Fruit-Animal combo is off-limits. Don't call your spouse Boo or use My Shorty/Tall-ey or anything else Justin Bieber might be tempted to use in referencing his girlfriends. And whatever Kim and Kanye decide to use when talking about one another, don't go there either. And on that same note, if Taylor Swift or new Disney stars begin using nicknames for their beaus, do not adopt them into your spousal vocabulary.

Also, do not turn your spouse's first name into something supposedly cool. Let Bob be Bob not Bobcat. Allow Misty to be Misty and not be Miss TnT. As well, do not ever combine your first names into a singular name as Jennifer Lopez and Ben Affleck once did—Bennifer deserved to die simply for that reason. Plus, Bartholomewlissa sounds like an infection.

Save your creativity and cleverness for other things.

On the flipside of cute is giving your spouse an evil nickname. There are too many to mention here. But any scatological or sexual curse word combined with any of their names, farm animals or body parts is off-limits.

And no, it does not make it better if you add a Mister or Mrs. or Sir or Madam to land in front of these sorts of names. If these sorts of names are your common tool for speaking about or to your spouse, it's time for a long-term counseling stint.

Finally, we come to giving names to private parts. Just let them be categorized like that—*Private* Parts.

Is it really that grand to have your breasts identified as if they were separate personifications? Does a penis need a first name? Do any of them need descriptors?

I think not. Let's retire nicknames, shall we?

Number Fifteen
Thou Shalt Not:
Justify a mood minefield

We all get in bad moods. Grumpy, whiney, grouchy, judging, obnoxious, offensive, negative and/or just overall unpleasant and basically unable to please.

But some spouses get in bad moods a lot more than others.

In fact, some spouses do not even emotionally own a *right side of the bed*. They are waking and walking and talking and breathing "bad moods" that will leave oil leaks and tire skids all over your day's driveway regardless of the weather condition.

Bad News: Spouses of such partners have failed in their quests for any sort of relational happiness. They went fishing for a marlin and instead pulled in an old boot that housed a family of angry Black Mambas; now they get to float on a pretty rough boat for a while.

But, there is a silver lining surrounding this storm cloud situation: When you have a spouse like I've described, at least you can count on his/her consistent fanged bitterness and rudeness and respond appropriately.

How, you ask?

Quality Disappearance: By joining Monday through Saturday night bowling leagues, knitting groups, Scrapbooking Collectives and/or Opium-Loving Pinterest Communes so you can be out of the house a majority of evenings. And maybe when you return home, your dark passenger will have already hit the sack. Then, ever so quietly, you can sneak in and look longingly at his/her sweet, subconscious face and be glad.

You can also be glad that you don't have the worst kind of spouse.

What kind of spouse could be worse?

One whose moods seemingly shift in a radical fashion from one side of the street to the other side and from paragraph to paragraph, being happy for one hour and then for no reason shifting into a moody blue so thick you cannot suffer it. These sorts of spouses are what I call *mood minefields*, because you never know if you are safe to be around them. Sure they might be huggy and positive and you want to be around them all the time as they emanate bright rays of love and light but then there is the unexpected huge BANG as you take a step onto the new mood that came out of nowhere. It's like walking and possibly even skipping through a meadow of plush grass, beautiful flowers and billowy clouds with giddy, gamboling sheep all around you and then stepping onto your spouse's mood mine as you are beginning to whistle the Andy Griffith theme song; your world is shifted into a frightening war time viciousness. The wondrous fields have turned into Vietcong territory, the leaping sheep have been sheared and slaughtered and you would only dare to whistle if you could think of how to grab the melody of *The End* by The Doors.

Thy kind and caring spouse from el paradiso must have just remembered the heavy punch line to a bad joke from childhood that made him feel like a dung-headed reject from Kazakhstan and is now folding his marital royal flush feelings in favor of some collapsing frowns, disappointed words and painful behaviors.

This unpredictability of mood is the worst because you cannot help but love being around your partner when she is on the shiny side of an affectionate and caring life, but then you prefer not to be there when the unseen mood mine gets stepped on. This leaves you with a problem. You cannot just go join a bunch of nighttime bowling leagues and alcohol-based affinity groups because then you might be missing the good times you've grown so pleased with. But, you also cannot handle the emotional volatility that comes with the spousal slingshot from one side to another.

So, what is to do?

I obviously think the onus is on the spouse who is throwing this *mood stick shift* into off-road eighth gear straight from first gear and causing a neck-jerking emotional whiplash for the partner.

My Advice to Minefielders:

> Go to a psychiatrist and find out if you have some sort of chemical imbalance that makes you act like this. Then take your North Pole/South Pole meds and hope really hard that you will not get destroyed by side effects or be transformed into an emotional zombie by the daily dosages.

> If you don't have a psychiatric issue and don't need any special meds, try to pay close attention to and make note of how many times you find yourself creating situations of uncomfortable emotional change for your spouse. (If you have a hard time noticing, I am sure your spouse can help you with that part.) Then once you see how often this mood minefield becomes reality and once you are able to understand the magnitude of the blasts, you can start asking yourself questions and taking directives such as the following:

> Is there a common denominator (circumstantial, memory-based, verbal trigger, physical state, etc.), which seems to be a lead-in to the mood shifts? If so, you could probably dig into whatever it is with a good therapist to see if you might at least learn how to avoid pressing that button.

With this sort of knowledge you would also be able to warn your spouse that you sense a mood mine about to arise. This would give your spouse time to become removed from the coming explosion so you can deal with it in a healthy way without affecting your relationship. So, it would go something like: Research, Realization, Trained Attention, Warning, Removal and finally, hopefully, No More Mine Fields. No more Vietcong. And no more Jim Morrison tunes.

Number Sixteen
Thou Shalt Not:
April Fool your spouse with something that will totally freak her out or cause him real worry

According to the doctors and the Mayan calendar, I was *supposed* to be born on April 1st but I faked my mom out and hung out inside that womb for an extra two days before swan diving for the exit. Still, despite my lateness, I was born to be a fool and have always loved April Fool's Day. Every year I found it to be great fun to arise early and catch someone off-guard with something shocking. As I grew older, I would amp up the complexity of my tales and challenge myself to fool those people who thought they could never be caught. I got a thrill out of turning someone inside out with an "acceptable lie."

But here is a good rule of thumb as it pertains to April Fool's Day and marriage: Do not ever try to pull off an April Fool's joke on your spouse that is going to be frightening or create true panic. Through counseling and by experience, I've found that spouses who avoid exposing their partner's gullibility to ridicule and who stop short of bringing them face to face with a terrifying possible truth for the sake of a laugh are more likely to be liked and trusted by their spouses. They are also less likely to be punched or slapped or ignored for weeks.

Here is a brief list of things you *should not* April Fool's your spouse with (especially if you are talented in theatre, own a great poker face, have friends who will help you and can access very believable props for "proof"):

◇ I'm pregnant (a faked pregnancy test and the ability to pop your belly out—not for men).

◇ I have inoperable cancer (breathless tears and a print out from the hospital).

◇ I gambled away our savings (move your savings into a new account your spouse does not have access to).

◇ I was texting and totaled the new car (send pic of a crushed car like yours).

◇ I just got fired for stealing staplers and Post-it Notes (have cardboard box of your work things and a drawer filled with staplers and Post-its).

◇ Billy (the 3-year old) just ate dog food and the rest of your Xanax pills (have babysitter call and a friend text from "poison control").

◇ Your dog just got hit by a motorcycle (fake blood on your hands and a newly dug hole in backyard).

◇ I have a second family I've never told you about (show a convincing scrapbook and plane stubs from Utah).

◇ Your dad had a heart attack/is in a coma (your mom is in on the joke and leaves a *verification voicemail*).

◇ I need you to bail me out (calling collect from a pay phone, crying and murmuring about manslaughter).

◇ I'm converting to Scientology (Tom Cruise memorabilia).

◇ If the cops call, I need you to tell them I was with you at the movies last night (frantic call and a quick hang up).

◊ Some people are coming to the house. Lock the door, get the gun and go to the basement (bowling friends who have trench coats ringing and banging on door—they might want to wear flak jackets).

*There are variations, and of course a bunch of others I have not listed here. You would be wise to keep yourself far from anything in the neighborhood of the above list. Ignore me at your own peril. And forgive me if I have given you some pretty good ideas as to how to pull these off. It's hard for me to give it up.

**By the way, my wife once smoked me big time on April Fool's Day. She totally convinced me that she had an encounter with aliens or something extra-terrestrial. She led it off by saying, "I know you won't believe me, especially today, but I've got to tell you something that happened to me on the way home and I don't know if I am going crazy or what…"

My wife is a kick-ass actress and her tears made it so believable. I was ready to kill E.T. wherever he was hiding.

***Final note: If you can pull off an alien-sighting joke with your spouse, feel free to do so. Also, any lottery winning ticket jokes are fine as long as you are ready to buy your partner some expensive item they have wanted for a long time, as evidence.

Also, if you use other dates/days on the calendar to "Punk" someone beyond the acceptable Ashton Kutcher-level, you'd better never do it to me.

Number Seventeen
Thou Shalt Not:
Be a Negative Forecaster

To forecast simply means "to predict." Weather forecasters predict the future weather, but they are usually not just making a guess about it by standing outside and looking around at the sky. Chief Meteorologists would never think of such a heretical practice. They are chief weather prognosticators because they have the appropriate education, local expertise, pattern recognition, historical precedents, and plenty of technology to show them the way to predict accurately; if you have never seen a Super Doppler 18,000 work its magic, then you have not lived well.

While it might now be disappointing to you that I am not going to segue into a discussion of the marriage mishaps of Chief Meteorologists, I must move on to my point, which has to do with a larger group of humans.

Robert DeNiro, I *am* talking to you. And all you spouses, I am talking to you, too. **Don't be a negative forecaster about life.** You do not have a Super Doppler in your possession. You are not gifted like Nostradamus. You do not have a time machine giving you insight into a future world run by time, chance, and the surprise freewill moves by capricious human beings. It is a fact that you don't know jack about what is coming down the road. You might be able to pull together some good odds based on some past behaviors, but you cannot say something will happen "without a doubt." There are no clouds in the life sky to guide you. No accurate barometers.

What does all of that mean?

You are no life prophet. You should not be predicting what is going to happen. You are totally welcome to make positive, optimistic guesses or even negative, pessimistic guesses.

But you do not need to act like you know, when you don't know.

Negative forecasters are those sorts of people who actually think they know what is coming and that what is coming is going to be very bad. They are hope-vampires, sucking on the necks of good possibilities and creating a radar map that promotes their worldview of negativity.

"Here is what's going to happen. We will go to dinner tonight. Then a wasting disease will strike me, which will set into motion a series of suicides and addictions among those we love. After this, a tsunami-level financial storm will hit the business we run and our kids will run amok as looters and pilferers and end up as juvenile delinquents. They will refuse to do their homework and be cast outside the educational system and probably become hired snipers. All of our friends will reject us. God will curse us and we won't go to Heaven."

Uh...please top seeing every current and future path in negative tones. Negativity weighs marriages down and negative forecasting typically is self-fulfilling. You want to put your faith in a terrible future and talk about it all the time like it is a given, prepare to meet up with some *version of suck.*

But don't drag your partner into your doomland.

For your partner's sake, read every Norman Vincent Peale book you can find. Get some powerful positive thinking pumping into your brain. Read the Bible, but not Ecclesiastes or Revelation for now. Don't hang out with compulsively negative people. And stop watching the news, reading the paper, or giving yourself any reason to believe in the negative forecasts you have been promoting for years.

Let the half-full glass exist. Hula-hoop in the front yard. Go on and let the sun shine in.

Number Eighteen
Thou Shalt Not:
Ask your spouse: "Are you really going to wear that?"

This question usually comes from a place of judgment. One spouse is saying to the other, "You have no taste, style, color distinction, understanding of where we are going and/or a vision problem if you think what you have chosen to wear is acceptable." By saying it, these people are not only ripping their spouses and making fun of them, but they are as well arrogantly claiming they know what looks best.

Are you Calvin Klein's stylist? Are you on the cover of GQ or Vogue?

If not, then don't disrespect the *closet fashion* of your partner.

Exception: If your spouse is wearing a half-shirt while donning Jordache products elsewhere, or if they have on one of those holey shirts from the 70's and clogs, you have my permission to waylay them.

Number Nineteen
Thou Shalt Not:
Be a Harangutan

Harangue—To lecture (someone) at length in an aggressive and critical manner.

Orangutan—Asian Great Ape with high intelligence.

Harangue + Orangutan = Harangutan

Harangutans are spouses who often resemble an annoying and dominant ape-like mammal when they begin verbally attacking their "loved ones" with intellectual critiques for a significant period of time, while using out of control body language and encroaching upon personal space with the red-faces of creatures bent on proving themselves right about something.

Does this describe you?

Are you a table-banging, chest-beating opinionator of a spouse who likes to dominate conversations with loud and long-winded monologues that are specially directed at your "obviously ignorant" significant other? Are you one of those people who live on a *soap box* and has put in so many of your *two cents* that you are forever in debt? Are you the know-it-all half of your marital coupling who thinks you need to turn every room of the house into a lecture hall where you can *adequately* "home-school" your spouse with nouns and verbs and adjectives and mostly crap statistics you have re-shaped to fit your purposes? Do you know *enough* about every subject possible *and* have such a deep insecurity that you have to elevate yourself above your partner (and maybe everyone else) with the use of your knowledge? Are you really the most sought-after Master of Profound Insights? Do you really think people are blown away by your ability to use GRE vocabulary within normal conversations? Are your rants about personality, idiosyncrasy, psychology, quantum physics, driving skill, housekeeping, political parties, sports excellence, sexual etiquette, religious correctness, etc., delivered in a rowdy, voluble manner and meant to make your husband or wife respond with only a nod or head shake? How do you react if you are challenged? Do you smile and thank your spouse for their input or do you go red-faced and scream your points on a louder repeat expecting thy loved one to submit silently to your AUTHORITYYY?

You might not think you are anything like the above. Most Harangutans don't think they fit the description and refuse to admit they are regularly acting ape-like in their discourses. But ask your woman or man and see what she or he thinks about it. Give them permission to speak freely and promise that you will not have a knee-jerk reaction. (If you've been behaving this way for a while, you have probably slowly taken away your partner's freedom of speech and created a timid mute who is afraid to open his or her mouth for fear of the Hulk with a Hitler-style speech showing up.)

If your spouse says that you are a Harangatun, then you have to ask for forgiveness, seek counsel, and possibly even wear daily duct tape on your lips until you can stop being only partially human in your discussions.

(Apologies to the Orangutans out there if I have offended you. I know you act better than most spouses on the planet, but the word harangue simply fit you best...)

Number Twenty
Thou Shalt Not:
Pick big fights with your spouse before some major stressful situation

You and your spouse are going to disagree. You are going to have fights with the one you love. Some of these fights are going to be over some really stupid topics while others are going to be about major issues. Reality is simple: you marry, you fight. Don't worry about it too much when it happens unless it gets personal or violent. Fights and abuse are two different things.

Anyway, some days you are going to be in one of those moods where it just feels right to pick a fight with your spouse. In other words, the fight between you and your spouse would not happen unless you actually grab onto something intentionally that you know is going to create boiling and cussing. The causes of this strange behavior are many. Maybe you wanted to slap your boss in the face earlier in the day but had to suppress the desire. Maybe you really had the urge to two by four the guy who tailgated you all the way home but decided it would be best to keep a clean police record for now. Then you get home and you think you need to blow off some steam, which leads you to pick a fight with your spouse. Or maybe you have been letting your spouse or kids get away with not doing their part with the housework for a long time and you are finally sick of it. So, you proceed to bring up a subject that you know will piss her off and you prepare for the verbal bare-knuckle brawl.

I pick fights with my wife. I talk about her trigger topics and watch the beast from beyond arise from the depths of her soul. And I enjoy the blowouts. I should not do it. But it helps, and she weathers it, because I weather it when she does the same type of thing. It's like a real-fake fight where we are sparring with Olympic headgear on. We break a solid sweat but we don't break any noses, either.

Okay, so that's reality. But here is some solid advice when it comes to picking fights: Don't push your spouse's buttons on purpose and get him/her all riled up, pressed against the ropes and embroiled in a fiery emotional beating before he/she heads to something important or stressful.

For instance, I know this motivational speaker who used to drive to some of his gigs with his wife, and his wife would not follow the above rule. Without fail, this woman (admittedly) would push her man's buttons and get him all worn out before he went out to speak. She'd basically press him against a trigger-spiked wall and he'd bounce off of it like he had been poked in the soul. He would defend himself and she would toss a grenade and he would respond with fury and she would dig a bit deeper and by the end of it, the guy was breathless, red-faced, mentally sliced, and had only five minutes until he took the microphone in front of a large crowd seeking to be uplifted by his gentle and powerfully positive charisma.

Imagine having to flip that switch and being able to do that job with energy, with authenticity and with a smile. The worst part of it all was that this guy was a motivational speaker for married couples who were struggling to keep their heads afloat. I'm sure it was never easy for him to push past the short-term memories of his own marriage junk waiting for him at the back stage door.

Fact is all of us have those calendar days ahead of us when we know it is going to be extra stressful for us. All of us have those upcoming days of hot sauce heat and painful pressure burning us up and weighing us down harder than the normal 9 to 5. You know you do. You know your spouse does. And even though it seems mega-obvious, you should have this conversation and make some sort of deal with one another to make sure you both hold off on starting some kind of *trigger your spouse spar session* on days where everything is going to be hard enough already. Cut each other some slack on most days anyway, but contract with each other to grant each other excess love and encouragement on those days when life is probably going to do its best to bang away at your unguarded chins.

If you do ignore this advice and you pick fights with your Pastor husband before he does a funeral for the mayor or start a smack down with your wife an hour before she defends her Ph.D. dissertation, you deserve whatever comes your way from the Karma Police.

Number Twenty-One
Thou Shalt Not:
Go off-scale

It's not your doctor's job to monitor your weight and keep you from Waffle Housing over one hundred added pounds during your marital life. Physicians do not have the only scales in town and you dare not checkity-check your lbs. only at the old yearly *white coat poke and prod.*

Here is some good advice for your marriage and your health: Get an accurate scale from Target and climb onto it everyday. Determine what a good range of poundage is for you to maintain and don't let yourself go outside of it. (A "good range" is not "somewhere from 175 to 325.")

Then monitor thyself daily. If you've moved up a bit from the day before, skip the $25 Venti Frappucino with extra sugar and caramel and avoid a carb or two and get the numbers back in your favor for the next morning. The less you weigh the next day, the more you can Supersize it at the following lunch time. I play this game on a seven pound range and after 18-years of being married, post-good metabolism and post-exercise, I am only seven pounds heavier than I was on the day I got married.

Hooray for me, right?

Well, let me say that when I don't scale myself daily, I can easily gain twenty pounds in two months without even trying. As has been said in plenty of other books, if you add on just one pound every month and do that consistently for 10 years, you will be 120 pounds heavier at that stage than you are now. That's not beach sexy. It's not office desk sexy. But even more importantly, it is not healthy. As a vital part of your family, you want to stick around aboveground for as long as you can and have some mobile quality of life along the way. As well, since weight gain causes so many medical issues, you want to stay away from having to spend your money on the expenses that come with the hospital industry. And besides financial costs, there usually comes a personal insecurity that arises every time you see your growth in the mirror and have to squeeze into your former wardrobe.

Don't do it to yourself, my friend. Stay on scale. Stay in range. Make mouth-wise decisions. And deliver thyself from the multi-level junk that comes along with the unmonitored life.

Number Twenty-Two
Thou Shalt Not:
Refer to your spouse's collections
as "stupid" or "childish"

While it may be your strong opinion that your spouse's *Star Wars figurine, Cabbage Patch Doll, vintage vase, or baseball cap* collection is the dumbest and most immature takeover of space in the world, you should keep it to yourself. Just because the one you love happens to love objects typically found in a toy box does not mean you should insist on an immediate removal. For some reason, she likes her collection enough to care for it and even add to it. So don't embarrass her for what you think is arrested development or a waste of energy/time/money.

To attack a person's valued collection is dangerously close to encroaching on a very deeply rooted individual hold onto symbols and past years. Collections typically carry emotional connections that cannot be explained, but should not be shamed.

That being said, if your spouse collects bongs, assault rifles, hair, deadly spiders and really anything Dr. Phil would frown upon, you can set boundaries.

As well, as the person sharing space in an egalitarian system of marriage, you have full rights to demand that his collection does not get a prime spot within the main living areas of the home/apartment/igloo. In other words, just because he has a Pink Floyd fetish, he is not entitled to paint the room in fitting tones and have an actual *wall* built in the den. He can keep his collection if it can be placed within a spare closet rather than being featured as the main décor in the kitchen and dining room. If the collection is or grows too big for a fair amount of room to hold, you are certainly allowed to demand that your spouse simplify from five Jabba the Hut Lego Play Sets to just one.

Another obvious allowance for you, the caring and compassionate and very understanding spouse, is to limit spending on this collection if it is a collection that can be added to. Set a fair budget for each other based on what you can easily afford and then you can both ask for additions for birthdays, holidays and anniversaries.

Oh and by the way, shoes and clothes and trophies and greeting cards are included in this "collectible" category. So think before you speak up about her collection if you happen to have a "collection" of your own...

Number Twenty-Three
Thou Shalt Not:
Hoard "random collections of junk"

While meaningful and properly-sized "collections" are allowed within marriage relationships, I strongly advise you not to become a hoarder who tries to disguise her/himself as a "collector of multiple meaningful items," which would be best described by most fair observers as random hodgepodges of old, broken, useless, molded, outdated, disorganized, and torn junk piles that are unworthy of placement on nickel tables at garage sales. While you may not ever reach the extreme levels of those who are featured on the syndicated TV show *Hoarders*, if you have multiple random collections of "stuff" best categorized by professional landfill owners and/or sane friends as "crap" or "trash," you are still a misdemeanor level hoarder who needs to quell your addiction to amassing material things that threaten to take up all the space in the house, garage, backyard, and numerous on-site and off-site storage sheds.

Once the "junk takeover" begins, it does not ever seem to stop until you've literally backed you and your spouse into a corner, leaving only one narrow walkway from room to room and from back to front door. I've seen this again and again. Collections of phone books and *National Geographic* magazines stacked up as half walls within real walls so guests can find their way to the bathroom without breadcrumbs. That is if someone dares go to the restroom, which is often overstocked with unused aquariums, stuffed animals, dying pets, cassette tapes, and Precious Moments figurines that are missing heads or hands.

This sort of junk-addiction hoarding can of course be hidden from would-be terrified guests if you can afford off-site storage sheds. I grew up watching this sort of off-site hoarding. My dad, who filled up the attic, both sides of the garage from ceiling to floor, every in-house closet, his "office," the back porch and two large backyard warehouses, never was stupid enough to encroach upon my patient mother's living spaces. But he was financially moronic enough to rent three huge storage sheds for twelve years, which cost our family over $15,000.

Smart investment?

When my father died and I was given the privilege of throwing away thousands and thousands of pounds of first generation computers, unnecessary work files, shredded tires, broken bicycles, incomplete weight sets, his weekly garage sale hauls of miscellaneous house wares, corrosive/explosive chemicals from his days as a chemist, years of magazines, bookshelves filled with dusty unread books, and of course the myriad carcasses of mouse families who lived amongst the ruins, I decided it was a fairly poor investment as well as a bad way to deal with a love of stuff. My dad, who was a super great, loving and generous guy, could have spent $5,000 on some *materialism therapy* and used the extra $10,000 ($15,000 if you include the costs of the junk he bought to fill up those sheds) to purchase Apple, Inc., stock (even Enron stock would have been interesting for a while). As well, he would not have wasted as much of his time/life, driven his spouse to serious frustration, and forced me to pull muscles and risk death in the unloading of his "valuables," which were already screaming *obsolescence* at the time of their storage.

Here is my final word on this: Don't let any sort of stuff come between you and your spouse. Whether the stuff is categorized as "junk" or still has its tags from a new shopping spree armload every week, it is not worth fighting about. Lay down your love of materials so they do not come between you and your life-lover—both literally and figuratively.

Oh yeah, and don't freeze your dead animals either. The freezer is for ice cream—not cats.

Number Twenty-Four
Thou Shalt Not:
Assemble IKEA furniture without your spouse in the room "navigating"

Rule: Both spouses must be present when IKEA furniture is being put together. Why? Because most cute furniture from IKEA comes unassembled, with a lot of random looking pieces and some very odd visual instructions that could fool even the handiest of humans. In my life, I have had the pleasure of putting together the same pieces of IKEA furniture several times after getting to the end of the directions and realizing I had the first piece of wooden bookshelf or chair or futon on backwards. (IKEA should at least include a glossary of Swedish curse words so I can make sure the inanimate objects understand me as I scream and threaten to splinter them with my hammer.)

Anyway, my wonderful wife never really understood why I was unable to complete such "simple tasks" on the first try and within an hour. After catching some sense of her feeling sorry for me because I was obviously proving myself to be a lower IQ mammal—on par with a manatee—I decided to do the mature thing and make her feel stupid about something else completely unrelated. If I were to be a manatee, she was to be an equally yoked sea-cow. So we fought about all sorts of things with the catalyst being a piece of Swedish furniture.

Then I figured out a better way - the way that I recommend in the above "Thou Shalt Not." When you put together IKEA furniture, put it together, together. One of you is the tool person and the other can be the navigator. But both of you are equally responsible for determining the proper steps, proper pieces and proper directions of the pieces. You must both concentrate together and not give your buy-in to any of the steps unless you are absolutely certain that you have figured out the specific Swedish torture-design. This almost always ensures that this cute piece brought straight from Hell will actually be put together correctly with minimal re-do, minimal cursing, and minimal fighting.

And if by working together, you can still never seem to get it together and you end up karate chopping vital pieces of the furniture in half, you will both be to blame and you will both get to have a hilarious story to share with others at dinner parties.

Shared frustrations can make the best memories. You win together. Or you lose together. Either way, there will be fewer manatee IQ glances and you will both have a funny tale to tell amongst your Swedish friends.

Author's note: This same principle applies to planning road trips or vacationing where directions are required. Make sure your spouse is right there with you as you look up highways, interstates, and side roads that will get you both to desired hotels, eateries, and attractions. Print out directions, check and double-check addresses, and/or put in GPS routes together. How many major fights, which lead to fear and erosions of trust, occur because one spouse did all the Google mapping while the other was doing the packing. Trust me on this one. If you do get lost or turned around on your way to a "relaxing" and "fun" destination, you want it to be both of your faults. This way you can both yell at Google Map failures rather than at one another.

Number Twenty-Five
Thou Shalt Not:
Pity yourself/Become "The Victim"

Almost everyone in the world is having a difficult time with something or someone. It is very rare for people to be experiencing complete bliss and ecstasy in every area of their humanity. One of the great and enduring truths of life is that the sun shines and the sun goes down bringing daily periods of darkness into play for everyone in a variety of circumstances—most of which are interconnected—making things at best partly sunny in all arenas.

Here is the point: When you have food poisoning, for example, it is sad and you are allowed to groan, but do not ever allow yourself to move into self-pity as if you were the only one experiencing a terrible day. It's foolish to cry out, "Why me?" and insist that others stop to offer you their tears when they need to save their reserves for themselves.

Self-pity, if indulged, can become a habit and lead to a life of being the constant victim—people who have determined that the world has decided to pull together its gang of troublemakers to focus on ruining their days—people who cannot see anyone else's pain and people who are a real pain in the butt to deal with in short encounters.

To the spouse who has the victim partner described above, set a firm boundary and refuse to indulge her self-pitying ways. Teach her the following self-talk: "Embrace the suck and shut up. Life is hard for everyone. I am not a lifetime victim. I won't blame anyone. I will not let myself be affected for long."

To the self-pitying spouse, learn the mantra above and say it to yourself every time you are about to start griping about your First-World problem or blaming someone else for making your life so "difficult." Get some perspective from those who don't have a glass half full or half empty, but instead carry positive attitudes and winning smiles as they suck in daily doses of chemo or watch their children starve because there is no food to be had or have had their limbs blown off by a landmine. They ain't got no glass, baby—unless it was part of a shrapnel-facial they got walking through a war zone.

Don't make your spouse despise you because you are such a wuss-case. Don't tempt your better half to turn you into a pity-party piñata. *Really listen* to your words and your tone and get some help in shifting them both if need be. Or don't change and see how many times your Superman and/or Wonder Woman pay attention to your cries for attention.

I know if I were a super hero and the same people were falling from the proverbial sky more than once a month, I'd probably let them break their noggins open to get myself a bit of super-peace.

I admit I have played the victim plenty. It is such an easy role to fall into and even easier to remain within. But it is not a place to stay if you want to be a good spouse and a good human.

Number Twenty-Six
Thou Shalt Not:
Bury your head in the sand during tough times

You are not an ostrich, even if people say you look like one.

So when troubled circumstances arise in front of you and your spouse, don't act like that flightless bird and burrow your head under the sand so you cannot hear or see the struggle for long. Don't leave your spouse hanging when the bills surprisingly get bigger than your income; when the kids get arrested for something juvenile (or worse); when their parents need a place to live for at least a year; when the car gets totaled or totally gives out; when your house is found to have black mold; when you both get fired; when the IRS calls for an audit; when your house is burglarized, etc. Do not disappear mentally, emotionally, and spiritually and simply remain physically present during the tough time.

In other words, do not literalize the cliché: When the going gets tough, the tough get *going*.

When the going gets tough, that's when two are better than one. An alliance in the midst of trouble gives you a better chance to overcome. But if you are a situational Houdini who will escape from every hard time, leaving your spouse to deal with what you refuse to deal with, you deserve chains, a water tank, and a hard punch to the appendix as Harry once did.

Stop being an escapist. Walk side by side with your spouse in the wind and waves. And don't run, because ostriches are pretty freaking fast.

Number Twenty-Seven
Thou Shalt Not:

Buy your spouse the following gifts for any occasion (unless specifically requested):

◇ Spanx

◇ Weight Watchers gift certificates

◇ A blank card with no money inside

◇ Plastic surgery *you* think is needed

◇ *Sex for Dummies* book

◇ Body waxing gift card

◇ A Rottweiler

◇ A black mamba

◇ World's Best Husband/Wife coffee cup

◇ A single one-way plane ticket to the Amazon

◇ Monster truck tires installed on her Prius

◇ A hit of Ecstasy

◇ His name written on a grain of rice

◇ A pillow stuffed with your own hair

◇ A life-size cardboard cut-out of you in your underwear

⋄ New dishwashing gloves, apron, and semen cookbook (Yes, it is a real cookbook and it is outselling this one...)

⋄ A spa day at Fantastic Sam's

⋄ Facebook/Twitter/Google+ emoticon-loaded shout-outs

⋄ A whoopee cushion and fart spray fun basket

⋄ A call-in bomb threat at her work so she gets the day off

⋄ A Native American headdress

Number Twenty-Eight
Thou Shalt Not:
Start sleeping nude unless agreed upon

Initial questions: Do nudists put clothes on to sleep? Do they feel the need to wear pajamas? Would *night socks* get you kicked out of one of their colonies?

Here's the lowdown on the main topic: If you start out your marriage by sleeping in the nude and your spouse is cool with it, I welcome you to just keep rolling your naked butt cheeks all over your 1000-count Egyptian wedding sheets. I am not going to judge you for your decision to *birthday suit* it all night long. If your bed is a return to The Garden of Eden for one or both of you, I say enjoy the coolness on your every square inch.

But if you are a pajama guy/girl or a simple underwear/panties and a tank human at bedtime you cannot/should not just one night choose to lose the basic body threads your spouse is used to you wearing and expect to not make them wonder about the sudden shift. Questions will arise: Is he wanting to have sex right now? Is she out of underwear, bras, panties, etc.? Has he been healed of "never-nudeness?" Is this a one-night experiment or are we going to have to get a King-Size bed to keep me at a distance? Did she read this suggestion in Cosmo or Bazaar (and if so, how do I cancel those magazines)?

I know it's not a super big deal in most cases.

But it can be a big issue if one spouse prefers there to be some coverage while the other spouse thinks it's time to leave the coverage to cornerbacks (fairly bad football reference). The spouse who is uncomfortable with the change usually thinks that an unspoken deal has been made for bedtime clothing and that this deal is being thrown out of the window. They might be uncomfortable with the change because they are modest or because they don't want your various "floppers" flopping around without some sort of control. Or maybe it is something else.

Either way, if you are thinking of clothes rebellion at night you need to get some sort of buy-in from your unsuspecting spouse. Or you need to at least let her know that you are going to try it out and give her a bed-nudity date. You also need to tell her what this new thing is all about. Give her some good reasons and maybe she will join you in a naked nightly spooning.

Just warning you that if you assume your spouse is cool with you doing this new cool trick, you might find that she actually feels extremely adamant about your putting your "things" away.

Number Twenty-Nine
Thou Shalt Not:
Yell across the house and expect your spouse to make the trek to you to hear some silly statement or to answer your questions

Do not be the spouse who is located all the way across the house, completely in control of his own mobility, thinks of something fairly unimportant (or at least something that could wait till later) and who repeatedly yells out at his partner to quickly leave behind her space (typically she is comfortably viewing TV or doing something important with the kids) so he can tell her his thoughts on some celebrity break-up or about what some other human told him at the grocery store early the week before.

Can you see how interrupting your spouse's peace and placement on a regular basis would create an increasing level of frustration? Are you able to recognize how your screeching, "Come here, babe," over and over when you are perfectly able to "go there" for a talk might lead to an explosive reaction? Are you able to note that distance, ambient noises, ceiling/floor fans, iPod music and/or television volume make it hard to hear you if you decide to go ahead and start sharing your nonsense information from the other room? In that instance, don't act upset if your spouse does not respond because if you do get angry, your spouse has every right to react with a "Here's Johnny" impersonation.

Here's my expert relational advice.

Quit being an ignoramus in a few simple steps:

First, think about whether what you want to say is at all relevant to your spouse. Second, if you decide that it is relevant, think about whether what you have to say needs to be shared in that moment or if it can be shared at a later time when you are together. Third, if it is a crucial piece of information or even a question you need an answer for immediately and your spouse is at a distance from you, get off your butt and walk to where they are. Fourth, if they are already engaged in something and should not be interrupted (learn to measure priorities), write a short note either sharing the question or the information or just put "urgent" on the piece of paper. Fifth, if your spouse is already available or becomes quickly available, tell him what is on your mind or what it is you think he needs to know. Sixth, do not expect your spouse to have any specific reaction to the information you pass on or to have a satisfactory answer to the question you are asking. Your spouse is not you and thus cannot be expected to think what you have said is that big of a deal. He might consider it trivial, but you cannot take that personally unless you enjoy arguing about stupid things. As well, your spouse is not always on his best attitude game and doesn't moonlight as an Oracle. So give him a break if he answers your question foolishly or in a manner that makes you feel a bit slighted. Having high expectations of your spouse is almost always a bad idea. In fact, some of the best counsel you could ever receive is to keep your expectations very low for every person, especially your life-lover. As I have written in other books, low expectations equal low disappointment.

Seventh, if you cannot handle the six steps mentioned above and you think like a lot of people do that it is your right to have your spouse jump every time you call-out, prepare for some extremely hard times. Either your spouse will come each time you call and build up some serious resentment and bitterness that will blow-out at some point or your spouse will start ignoring you and cre-ating a distance that neither one of you will be able to cross.

You need to be humble and remember that you are in a partner-ship rather than on top of a monarchy. You also need to carry that humility into your thoughts and recall that just because you have a question or some bit of information to share, does not mean that you need to form words around the thought or questions. Your news interruptions and your curiosity, if overdone, can be infuriating enough to kill more than cats.

Number Thirty
Thou Shalt Not:
Auto-Correct your spouse

Don't you think it is annoying when your "Smart Phone" auto-corrects you and "fixes" your texts when you just want to communicate a simple statement to someone else? I've actually punched my phone in the face for turning my words into other words I did not want it to mess with. I am not a fan of auto-correction.

Same goes for relationships. Being the auto-correcting "Smart" Spouse who always feels the need to fix the words of a significant other when that significant other has no desire for your correction in conversation is mighty angering.

I mean, do you really have to interrupt your spouse and auto-correct her version of a funny anecdote she is sharing? Does every detail of a story have to be exactly correct? Can you allow for some embellishment and hyperbole or do you have to stop your spouse and basically shame her for not telling it exactly how it really was? Can you give some slack when it comes to forgetting things?

Is it vital that every vocabulary word be perfectly pronounced or even properly used by your spouse if in their communication they got close enough that the majority of the people around understood where they were going? If your spouse reaches for a GRE word and comes down with a GED word, do you actually need to chuckle at him and let everyone within listening range know that you caught the mistake and know what should have been said?

Advice: Unless your spouse has asked you to help him speak with eloquence and accuracy in any and every venue and has specifically asked you to auto-correct him if he makes any sort of conversational mistake, it's best to just keep your mouth shut. You have not been given permission to get involved as an auto-corrector for some good reason. Can you respect thy spouse's piehole?

Exception: Now, if your spouse is spouting major offensive, racist, sexist, anarchist and/or politically incorrect phrases bordering on treason, you can certainly feel within your rights to shut him up, apologize to the crowd, and drag him away.

Number Thirty-One
Thou Shalt Not:
Be nicer to strangers, acquaintances, and other people's spouses than you are to your spouse

This one happens all the time but it should not - Couples who treat each other like trash, but then turn immediately around and are as sweet as can be to the people around them. What an ugly charade and façade—the kind that makes the outside world say, "Oh, that Jenny is so great and kind and loving. I bet Bob is so happy he has her as his wife," but makes those who know better say, "What a fake chick—why hasn't Bob killed Jenny yet?"

Or maybe it is Bob who is the bitchy one.

It goes both ways and it makes me sick. I've done it a few times myself. I've treated my wife like crap and then walked into a Starbucks and treated the baristas like superstars (which they are at my neighborhood SB). What a joke. The one I love gets my cruelty and the ones I barely know get my smiles and tips. This has also happened when hanging out with our married friends. I am Mr. Penis to my wife in the car, but then when we step into the sushi bar, I become a winking flirt to the other spouse and a loving, understanding brother to the husband. Ugly behavior that should not go without punishment.

See the movie *Who's Afraid of Virginia Woolf?* if you need a visual of what I am talking about here. (And best not to follow the on-screen or real-life patterns of the main actors, Richard Burton and Elizabeth Taylor.)

Number Thirty-Two
Thou Shalt Not:
Watch the following movies on romantic date nights

◇ Dancer in the Dark

◇ Eraserhead

◇ Gigli

◇ Gentlemen Broncos

◇ Pi

◇ Kill Bill 2

◇ Anything with Jean-Claude Van Damme

◇ Masters of the Universe

◇ Deliverance

◇ Anaconda

◇ The Break-up

◇ Borat

◇ Old Yeller

◇ The Shining

◇ Naked Lunch

◇ Pink Floyd The Wall

◇ In the Company of Men

◇ Happiness

◇ Full Metal Jacket

***While *some* of the movies above are really good flicks, they just don't seem to spark the flame and romantic fire for either male or female. If you are looking for an anti-aphrodisiac though, most of these will work just fine for that purpose.

Number Thirty-Three
Thou Shalt Not:
Be An Overly Busy Human

If you buy into the ideal of BUSY-NESS as most of us good and stupid Americans do, you will pack your daily, weekly, and monthly schedules so tight that those around you will be satisfied by your breathless attempts to achieve every *have-to* thrown your way and thus be impressed that you are not one of the foolish American Idles. Oh, the *have-to's*. You know them well don't you?

"I have to do this before tomorrow."

"I have to get this list done now."

"I have to buy the new iPhone as soon as it comes out."

And since these things are phrased in this way, there really is no room for discussion or option.

Have-to equals obligation.

Most of the *have-to* things promoted in our culture are task-based and project-based high-expectation to-do lists that come with logistical demands and looming deadlines. They are rarely of the relational and restful sort. Typically, relational *have-to's* are considered culturally optional. Thus, we neglect our need for quality time spent with our spouses and/or with our kids. We trade in these amazing opportunities because we have bought into the idea it's best to be moving around at a fast pace doing supposedly important things, when actually these "important" things will not be remembered beyond the year.

As mentioned in the last book, if you have two busy spouses in a marriage, they will typically rush a cheek kiss and wave a quick goodbye as they go on to their next *have-to.* They might bemoan their schedules once in a while, but because The Rat Race is an acceptable conformity they cannot complain. It is how everyone else is doing it and thus how they will do it.

In this mad rush, spouses lose one another as human blurs within their scenery. Love does not move fast and cannot exist but on a respirator within this type of marriage. Spouses become excellent bill-paying partners but they cannot continue to go deep with each other by taking a once a year vacation to Hawaii in an attempt to re-connect.

You can see this cultural damage being passed on as married couple parents begin teaching this busyness to their kids from an early age. Individuals are supposed to be busy no matter what their age—so kids are morphed into pre-pubescent do-ers as they are enrolled into dance, gymnastics, baseball, football, soccer, language learning and every other crazy busy opportunity. They are taught to be like mommy and daddy. Work when you work and then work when you play and the sleep will come when the lactic acid build-up just takes over.

And at the end of the day, relationships within a family are built around stressful attempts at success within various venues instead of built around slowed-down meals at a table at which encouragement and listening dominate.

In response to busyness, I want to encourage all of us to reconsider what actually *has* to be done and then remove those things which will not add to our relationships with spouse, with children, or with friends. Create some space. Allow others to perceive you however they like as you leave blank spots in your calendar. Be brave enough to be one of the un-busy.

If you do not kill busyness and find a way toward a schedule with many empty spaces left there for the real *have-to's*, busyness will kill you and every relationship you have.

By the way, it has to be a conscious decision to slaughter this cultural conformity on a daily basis. Hoping for extra time to magically appear is a foolish hope.

Number Thirty-Four
Thou Shalt Not:
Screen your spouse's calls or ignore their texts during the day

I am a bad boy when it comes to screening and ignoring calls and texts from just about everyone. But at least I am consistent. I blow everyone off until I feel like returning the multiple communication attempts. And it does not mean that I am mean. It just means that I am an emotionally complicated person who only has so much communication to give out on a certain day.

BUT, I *ALWAYS* RESPOND TO MY WIFE'S CALLS AND TEXTS.

Even if I am feeling especially emotionally complicated, mentally exhausted, and limited in my communication abilities, I will get back to her as soon as I can. Why? Because she is my spouse and thus deserves preferential treatment. I know she is probably not calling because she is in some emergency situation. She probably just wants to tell me to grab some organic almond butter on my way home. Or maybe she wants to offer some well-intentioned but unsolicited advice. No matter. I value her and want her to know that her communications take precedence over almost anything.

This does not mean I immediately return her calls if I am having a meeting with a client, doing relationship counseling, or making diplomatic headway with North Korean leaders. But since I am interested in what she has to say above all others, I make it a point to get back with her.

Now, does she do the same for me? No. But she also knows I usually have annoying and sarcastic comments for her that are actually meant for my own self-entertainment. Plus, her phone is not with her 24/7 like mine is and she actually has very important tasks to complete if she is going to become the next Head of the United Nations, as has been proposed by some dictator in Honduras.

Anyway, I shan't beat this dead animal any longer. Just make it a priority to reach out to your spouse during the day in some form or another and if they reach out to you, do not shun their call or text or make up some excuse as to why you did not receive it.

Number Thirty-Five
Thou Shalt Not:
Be an Overly Entitled, High-Expectation Human

If we buy into the idea that we have rights to happiness, we tend to act entitled to what makes us happy. What makes us happy is typically determined by what we desire and thus we set our life expectations based on what we want. If these entitlements/expectations are not met with regularity, we lean into disappointment and tend to react like a child who does not get his way. A simple way to say it is that we are First World and First Class Spoiled people. We all *want what we want* and this attitude spills over into our marriages.

When we have high expectations of our spouses, we tend to put a lot of pressure on them to do what will make us happy in every area. And since there are about one hundred potential expectations within a marriage on a daily basis, this can mean a lot of disappointment if and when spouses are not willing/not able to hit the marks that make us happy. This leads to various responses, most of them meant to ultimately get what we want from our spouses: tantrums; demands for better treatment/action; threats; emotional and physical manipulations (aggressive and passive-aggressive); tit-for-tat takeaways (e.g., better sex for a cleaner kitchen); comparisons to other spouses; control/attempt to re-shape a person into a "better" mold; shopping for a different spouse who might be able to spoil us as we are used to (the constant pursuit of a happiness-giver); etc.

Most people will not admit to being like the spouse described above, because it sounds so ugly and, well, is so ugly. But just because we avoid admission does not mean we are not at least partially ugly. I have seen it in so many marriages and often from both sides of the same marriage that it would be hard to imagine that most of you reading now do not fit into this tendency. I know that I certainly fit into the tendency.

I have been taught to have high expectations in every area of life—from my car and my computer's performances (both inanimate objects I have yelled at and even physically abused like they have purposefully let me down) to my waiter and my imaginary dog, both who had better come when I call. So of course I am going to take this sort of ugly expectation home with me and demand plenty of satisfaction from my wife, whom I married to be my helper towards happiness.

I suggest everyone reading this right now to think about how much expectation you have of your machines, your pets, your co-workers. your entertainment, your kids, and most of all, your spouse. Consider how you respond when these people and things do not live up to your expectations. If your spouse does not feed you something you want, satisfy your sexual urges with the proper moaning and groaning, listen to you as carefully as you would like, treat you with respect in public, say the right sorts of things about your ideas, encourage you as you need, leave the toilet in the right position, etc., how do you react, especially if such things are not done habitually? Are you disappointed? Do you make waves? Do you try to spur your partner on to become more like you want? Have you thought about finding someone who might be a better option?

My take: Happiness—you do not deserve it. You have no right to it. The Constitution of the U.S. of course tells you that you are entitled to pursue it. But in pursuing it, you just might crush your lover with the expectations you've been told to add to the pursuit. How about taking the pursuit of happiness out of the picture and instead work on/focus on helping others climb up by serving them? How about pursuing other people's happiness? How about doing your best to pursue your spouse's happiness?

If we can get this idea through our thick, spoiled, entitled skulls and become servants to our spouses, satisfied by joy rather than by an American ideal, our marriages will have a chance. In fact, I believe by shifting our pursuit we will even find ourselves walking in that daily happiness we had so desperately tried to create the other entitled way.

Number Thirty-Six
Thou Shalt Not:
Be A *Shop for More* Human

The ideal of *More* has always been a problem for the human race. For you Bible people, from the time of Adam and Eve, where the first of us humans got to hang out with God in a perfect place and with perfect conditions/circumstances, we have been tempted and have then fallen for the offers of More. (If you are an evolutionist, replace Adam and Eve with Amoeba and Tadpole who tried to get *More* out of their undeveloped existence.)

We may have everything we have ever wanted, but if we can get more, we will try to grab it even if it costs us what we already have. And we do not just want more, we want more now. The quicker, the better. Forget that it is unnecessary and that we cannot afford it; jam it on the credit card and soak in the dopamine release of debt growth in the name of materialistic pursuits.

Face it. We have been trained to be Shoppers. Our eyes have been instructed to ever be on the lookout for a conquest—a discovery of something new that will massage our cravings for at least a short while. Malls exist because we are never satisfied with what we have. TV ads chisel away at our contentment and convince us to look upon what we have with disdain. We see our lives in a dim shade of First World scarcity and listen for any version of the excuse calling us to sell the old version, which works perfectly fine, so that we can have the more and better as soon as possible.

Bigger screens, nicer phones, golf clubs for five extra yards, larger houses which require new furniture, Apple addiction Pads, the Lexus upswitch—there is plenty to put us in the middle of world-love and credit card debt sweat.

There are two problems with this for marriages: One is the debt part, which puts a constant pressure on both partners to make enough money to make minimum payments. If a job is lost, fights usually increase as bills pile up. We might be surrounded by items that are daily depreciating in value, and our neighbors might nod and smile at our ability to shop and stay in style. But when divorce leads to a division of these things, they don't quite seem worth it. Nor does the debt that stays with us till death us do part.

The second problem with this is how the shopper mindset comes against marriage. Many humans will scoff at this forthcoming idea, but those humans are worthy of flogging and should be ignored.

What's the idea behind the Negative Shopper Mindset?

If you tend to be on the lookout for the new and better products and if you are usually focusing on what you don't have rather than on what you do have, you will tend to do the same things relationally. You might have a spouse already who has some relatively good traits, but the problem is that she has been hanging in your closet for some time now. She has aged. She is the same beautiful article, but because she has been draped on your shoulders for so long, you look past her and take her good fit for granted. She was your favorite shirt at one point, but she does show signs of wear and tear and you have discovered small frays around her hem. Plus monogamy is not necessarily in style, so, your eyes go on the lookout for a new possibility. There is a tendency to window shop and then to wonder "what if." This window shopping is sometimes followed by a spouse actually stepping into the store where an attraction has drawn them inside. Then there is a browsing and a look in the mirror and then possibly a *trying-on* of someone new in a private space with little consideration of cost or future itchiness.

Truth: Shopper People who want more now tend to extend this tendency into their relational closets and end up with several unsatisfactory wardrobes, lonely days, and an empty wallet.

Don't let yourself go this route. Avoid Buyer's Remorse when it comes to your marriage. When you say "I Do" you must remove all tags from your spouse and throw away all receipts so you cannot return them at some future point. People who don't do this and go instead with a sort of Wal-Mart marriage purchasing plan, knowing they can always take their husbands or wives back to where they discovered them are emotional and carnivorous consumers who feed on souls. That sounds pretty bad, right? Good, because people actually doing this sort of thing suck.

Number Thirty-Seven
Thou Shalt Not:
Point the remote control at your spouse and repeatedly say "Mute, Mute, Mute"

For one thing, this action will not actually work so it counts as a waste of your valuable energy, which you could have used later to make it from the couch to the refrigerator one more time. Conserve!

Second, by doing this, you have just expanded what could have been a semi-short conversation into a massive hour-long argument about what a crappy person you are to "treat him/her as such an insignificant other." Unless you are an argument lover, this makes you a time-wasting idiot.

Third, whatever your insulted partner says in response to your action will be considered fair, accurate and true, because only jerks, freaks, a-holes, and/or wanna-be single people tell their spouses to shut up over and over so they can watch some dumb television show that is probably recording on TiVo. (If the TV is actually off when you do this, it's worse because you are saying you would rather stare at a blank screen than have him share something with you about what he thinks is presently important.)

Fourth, recognize you have leapt from gentle person over the passive-aggressive line and have entered the direct aggression mode of addressing your mate. By crossing these lines, you are stopping just short of strangling your spouse to keep him from annoying you.

Where is this bad behavior coming from? It's possible you have some bitterness and resentments built up toward him that might need some professional counseling or a Catholic Exorcism to bring you back to humaneness.

(It's also possible this is not entirely your fault. It's quite possible that your spouse has slowly dragged you over your fairly wide lines of gentle responsiveness and into this cruel activity using intentional or unintentional forms of grating *Chinese water torture-like techniques* modeled to him by his parents.)

Question:

Does every stupid and seemingly unending sentence about topics you cannot stand slip from his mouth like a drip, drip, drip, drop, drip, drip, drippity, drop, droppity drip and hit you solidly on your nervous system sending you into a maniacal state of mind?

A good response:

If your spouse *is* consistently interrupting your relaxation and entertainment times, scream as if inside of a scream chamber, learn to power vomit and cry on cue, and see if he gets the subtle hint he is doing something, which is putting you in asylum territory.

Number Thirty-Eight
𝕿𝖍𝖔𝖚 𝖘𝖍𝖆𝖑𝖙 𝕹𝖔𝖙:
Release your spouse's pet into the wild and then act as if you don't know what happened to it

I like animals and most SeaWorld creatures.

But I don't like making these animals into pets. I do not like pets of any sort.

Having a cat, dog, reptile, bird, fish, baboon, spider, and/or any sort of non-human entities moving around in my place of residence or in the backyard of my residence makes me very uncomfortable. I do not mind the zoo now and then. But the idea of taking care of anything with a heart and a lifespan makes me want to dive out of a high building.

I'm not saying I am right in my dislike of pets, but I choose not to have one because I do not want to feed, bathe, and/or pick-up after it.

I also do not want to become accidentally emotionally attached to some hairy beast or scaly creation I have been required to name. Once I give something a name and clean up its poop, I'm pretty much hooked on it and will probably fall in love with it.

A lot of people feel the same way I do with regards to being anti-pet, but they end up falling in love with someone who already owns a pet she will not part with post-wedding. Your spouse has bonded with a furry or scaly thing that usually has bad breath, problems holding onto its skin and is extremely jealous of your new position in the home (it probably has plans to kill you while you sleep.)

So, what's to do?

Well, the answer is definitely not to wait for your spouse to go to work as you fake sickness so you can drive the abovementioned pet to the busiest highway in your area and release it into traffic. And it's also not okay to take it to the pound. Or to a forest 100 miles away. You just cannot do any of these things or anything in the vicinity of such actions. Have you read Poe's *The Tell-Tale Heart*? This would be *The Tell-Tale Bark* (or Meow or Slither or Hop). And it would not end well.

Advice: Don't date anyone who loves pets if you do not love pets. Unless you want to get smothered by his pet as you sleep or unless you are cold hearted enough to betray your spouse by endangering his best friend.

Number Thirty-Nine
Thou Shalt Not:
Go to the following spots for romantic dates:

◇ World Wrestling Federation event

◇ Marilyn Manson concert

◇ Wal-Mart Café and shopping night

◇ A burlesque show

◇ The Holocaust Museum

◇ Chuck E. Cheese

◇ A Swinger's Club/An Adult "Key" Party

◇ A brewery tour

◇ Sherwin Williams

◇ A slaughterhouse

◇ A Scientology Audit

◇ The stage play, *Equus*

◇ *Rocky Horror Picture Show* with audience participation (but it's so fun)

◇ The funeral home to casket-browse

◇ Gay Pride parade

◇ Local Comic-Con

◇ The National Spelling Bee (early rounds)

◇ Nursing home Bingo Domination Night

◇ Any amusement park situation where vomiting is likely

◇ A nude beach

◇ The circus

◇ Benny Hinn and Rod Parsley "prosperity & healing" twin bill

◇ A storage auction

◇ Garage sales

◇ Public beheading

◇ All-day street gang convention

Conclusion:

Marriage is an amazing thing. But it is not an easy thing. The majority of the best and most successful couples I have known/worked with over the years have been to the brink of separation and/or divorce on several occasions.

That's right.

Strong couples with ten-plus, twenty-plus and even thirty-plus years of commitment history stand at the edge of the relational boxing ring ready to throw in the towel and stop the fight for their forever-love because too much *current bad* has seemingly trumped the *initial good*. The pains, betrayals, neglect, annoyances, idiosyncrasies, losses, and straight-up human mistakes brought them to the edge of calling it quits before they backed off, worked on a two-way solution and pressed on toward a better ending.

That's something I want everyone who reads these books to consider: Marriage is hard for everyone. It's a wonderful AND terrible walk with others who are not the perfect people you thought they once were or the well-crafted people you thought they might become. Marriage takes perseverance and it takes acceptance and it takes your dying to your entitlements and expectations. It requires selflessness and patience. Marriage can grow you into a mature human who is clothed in an attitude of kindness, humility, and support. It can teach you to be an unflappable lover, loyal ally and grace-giving person.

There is beauty in that, my friends.

But it is a beauty you must work for and pray for rather than shop for and claim.

Final Words: May your "I Guess I Do" become "I Really Do."

'Til death do you part.

Eighteen Valentine

She is the blend of day and night

The only troop on either side of me

Ever the warmth yet a steel vocal

When I try to race away to ruin

When I mistake us into forced undoing

She boils until she bubbles then she loves

Like swells and tides, she loves

Hammers have pounded into us

Ones we have held and ones we have not

But flattened hopes still breathe

Where life smells of caution in the new, old land

Deceiving us with a double promise

It stretches onward without ripples but holds a secret I think we've found

You'll go away to the edges and come back around

I know her and she knows me deeper and deeply

We take turns carrying the other's heart through dark

How could this valentine ever be blue?

She wants for me to live more than I do

I want for her to go farther than the sand drawn line

This is why we ally, sigh, and smile

Through the valley deep troughs of time

To my person, past the pasta and the moves

Beyond the things others call the wheels and the glues

My famous love, I've got every best end to every deal

When I keep my eyes on that frame of you.

Marital Food Poisoning

I actually ate it because the meal sounded fantastic when I read its description and saw its corresponding picture on the menu. It was well-marketed. Then it lived up to its billing as it was brought smoking hot from the kitchen to my table. It smelled incredible as it was placed in between my fork and my spoon and just under my nose. It even tasted as great as it smelled and made me exceedingly glad I ordered this particular dish because it was seemingly perfect for me. I took in as much of it as I could possibly ingest and felt that the price I paid for it was totally worth it, despite its high cost.

But after I left the restaurant and as hours passed, my stomach began to alert me that this seemingly perfect choice, while initially grand, was going to be a cruel punishment leaving me fairly helpless on my bathroom floor. From that humble spot, I cursed that perfect dish. I cursed the waiter for recommending it and the menu maker for making it look and sound so good. I cursed myself for ordering it. I should not have believed its multi-sensory pull. I should not have committed to it so completely. Now, my whole being felt the effects of its curse. Every part of me quaked and weakened as my mind tried everything it could do to launch it out from every possible exit point. I just wanted to be free from its hold.

It was marriage food poisoning and it wasn't going anywhere.

Gambling with Love

Marriage is a major gamble with pretty terrible odds. In fact, if marriage were a casino game, I'd compare it to a slot machine which has a cool, flashing neon sign playing enticing music and featuring a theme that tempts you to take a seat and stare at the triple wheel in front of you. And of course it would be the most promising slot machine, which advertised potential Mega-Bucks that would bring life-changing rewards and joy-making times in every paradise on the planet.

But in reality, it would also be the one that takes whatever investment you put into it and delivers nothing except for some exciting spins, a sore wrist, and growing desperation to just break even.

 Marriage is a machine almost everyone tries to Jackpot from. It's a machine almost everyone goes broke in front of. And it's a machine that gives you enough back to keep you putting more in until you have little left to do, but cash out.

Are you sure you ought to play?

About the Author

Ben Donley, author of several books and essays, has many years of experience as a husband and as a Spiritual and Relational Advisor for those at every stage of the marriage process. Ben is now Head of Acquisitions and the Creative Director for **Jock and Lola Publishing** (Los Angeles and West Texas) and hopes his writing will help some humans both know better *and* do better.

For speaking engagements or consulting appointments, contact Ben at:

Phone: 310-770-2061

http://www.bendonley.com

www.ingramcontent.com/pod-product-compliance
Lightning Source LLC
Chambersburg PA
CBHW020005290326
41935CB00007B/307